Epping Forest was saved for the metropolis and the nation in 1871-4, by simple assertion of the rights of common inhering in the local inhabitants. But Kinder Scout, Bleaklow Head, the Langsett, Saddleworth, and Yorkshire moors were in different case. Those barren tracts never had the abundance of pasture, where the commoner could graze his beasts, or of woods and spinneys, where he had the right to gather firing; hence the claims to commonage were unimportant. Thus, the moorlands remained waste lands out and out, and nobody troubled much about them. So far as access to them was concerned, no let or hindrance was interposed by heedless landowners. Those who wanted to could cross them where they pleased from village to village, but they were very few who did so please; and as to recognised routes, the only ones of any extent were the ways followed in the time before railroads by the great droves of cattle that used to be sent from north to south.

Then, one unlucky day, grouse-shooting became a pastime with the idle rich, and the policy of shutting up the open wild gradually began. Nobody was as yet alive enough to the charm of these vast solitudes to raise objection. Only in the last few decades have the public realised the seriousness of their loss. Now, however, it is becoming at length an obvious fact, and we wonder how our fathers could have failed to appreciate it, that the open spaces of the Pennine are the back garden, the recreation ground, for the crowded millions of workers in the adjoining towns. They are to the big industrial cities of the north what the commons, heaths, and downs of the Home Counties are to London. Complete freedom of access may be delayed, but it will come inevitably; the day surely cannot be far off when every barrier must be removed, to meet the lawful necessities of the people.

Extract from "The Forbidden Land – A plea for public access to mountains, moors and other waste lands in Great Britain" by Ernest A. Baker, published in 1924.

THE 1932

KINDER TRESPASS

A personal view of the
Kinder Scout Mass Trespass
by Benny Rothman

Willow
PUBLISHING

Dedicated to the memory
of the late Howard Hill.

First edition 1982

© Willow Publishing 1982
ISBN 0 9506043 7 2

Willow Publishing
Willow Cottage, 36 Moss Lane
Timperley, Altrincham
Cheshire, WA15 6SZ
England

Printed in Great Britain by
The Commercial Centre Ltd.
Hollinwood, Oldham

Contents

Foreword

I'm proud to be a Mancunian. I was born nearly 50 years ago within cheering distance of United's ground at Old Trafford. But not until my family moved from Manchester's grime to wartime Glossop did I discover the sombre majesty of Kinder Scout.

We were a poor family. Mum lovingly stitched together for me a rucksack made from silver barrage balloon material. And I saved the pence from my paper round until I could afford a tent . . . well, three-quarters of a tent! It had no door and I used to pitch it on Kinder with its back to the wind and rain. Newspapers and towel were my groundsheet, hobnailed boots my pillow. Supper was boiled potatoes doused in Oxo; I was lucky to have any breakfast at all.

I would clatter over the Snake road or up Chunal Hill to the breezy uplands of Kinder, my promised land. I would camp by the Mermaid's Pool (no national park wardens to shoo you off in those days), scramble on the mucky, wet rocks around the Downfall, wander along the airy edges or get lost in the boggy morass and peak hags of the plateau.

They were happy, carefree days . . . except for one thing. To help boost my meagre equipment I took a school holidays job as a grouse-shooters' beater. With my Glossop school pals I would line up waving a white flag and scare the hapless grouse towards the shotguns peeping above the shooting butts. And I'll never forget the nausea – the sheer, sickening horror – of seeing gamekeepers, fellow beaters and our employers picking up "winged" grouse and banging the birds' heads against boots to finish them off. A merciless "sport" is grouse-shooting . . . if you can call it a sport, that is! Truly, Man is the cruellest animal of all.

Happily for me, however, that job as a beater was short-lived. One day in the Peakland mist I got lost in a wilderness of heather and peat groughs. Somehow I emerged between a line of beaters and executioners. The grouse spotted me, did a U-turn over the beaters' heads . . . and the gunmen didn't slay a single victim on that drive. For the first and only time in my life I heard the classic words "You're fired". The gamekeeper paid me off with ten bob and I returned to Glossop thankful that I no longer had to take part in the carnage.

Eventually my family moved to Wythenshawe. My love affair with Kinder continued, only this time I took the bus from Manchester to Hayfield to tramp past Edale Cross and shred my hands on the rough gritstone buttresses above Grindsbrook.

And it was on the top deck of the bus back to Mosley Street one wet Sunday night that I first heard *The Manchester Rambler'* sung . . . and heard of the historic Mass Trespass of April 24, 1932.

Years afterwards I met the likeable Bernard Rothman – "spelt like the cigarettes," he told me. A smiling, intense, enthusiastic man is "Benny", the rambler who inspired and led the Mass Trespass just a few months before I was born. He told me of the ramblers' gathering in that derelict quarry on Kinder Road, Hayfield, the defiant march by idealistic young men to the jealously-guarded grouse moors, the scuffles with gamekeepers and the court hearing which turned almost into a political trial. With two brigadier-generals, three colonels, two majors, three captains and two aldermen on the jury what chance did a 20-year-old working-class lad from Manchester and his pals stand?

But Benny stuck to his guns – and went to jail for his principles of the freedom to roam Kinder and other open spaces. While one might not agree with his politics, there's no denying that it was his fight and similar demonstrations – with the publicity which they attracted – that led to today's freedom to enjoy Britain's national parks.

Much remains to be done. Only recently I have been hustled by farmers from the forbidden Aran Hills in Wales. I have wandered off the permitted routes over Lancashire's Bowland Fells, with the slight uneasiness which spoils a day in the country. I have brushed with landowners and shepherds in the great wide spaces of Scotland. Clearly, Benny's battle on behalf of outdoorsmen must continue, even 50 years after.

This book then, told in Benny's own words, is an important historical document for the rambling world. It teaches a lesson which every rambler must never forget. It is a book to buy, keep . . . and cherish.

Tom Waghorn

Tom Waghorn is a prominent Manchester journalist, a regular contributor to Climber and Rambler magazine and a member of the Outdoor Writers Guild. He helps to promote the work of the British Mountaineering Council and is in the Rucksack Club and Climbers' Club.

Acknowledgements

I would like to thank Cicely Marsh, Roger Hubank, Maurice Levine and Harry Rothman for their advice; Ruth and Eddy Frow, S. Clairmonte, Kenneth Warrender, Harold Colley and Judith Warrender for their assistance; Harmony Music Ltd.; The Peak Park Planning Board, H. Minshull, Lance Helman, Manchester Central Reference Library, T. H. Woodward and Keith Warrender for permission to use photographs; Beatrice Randles and Betty Harris for typing.

The maps on pages 13 and 14 are reproduced by permission from 'Trespassers Will Be Prosecuted" (1934) by Phil Barnes.

The author retracing the route of the Trespass, April 1981.

Introduction

Fifty years have passed since the Mass Trespass on Kinder Scout took place. With the passing of time, the dulling of memories, and the deaths of many of those who took part in the trespass, a whole mythology has grown around the Trespass.

Even at the time of the trespass itself, there were as many versions as there were newspaper reports, and since 1932 many and often contradictory accounts have arisen.

I have written this book because of this, and because I believe that the Mass Trespass is too important to be dismissed either as youthful folly, or as a political stunt.

I have interviewed participants, local villagers, keepers and policemen who took part. I have re-read newspaper accounts of the time, and again looked at the court proceedings, in order to present as accurate an account as possible of the trespass, and what brought it about.

The book could not be published at a more appropriate time. Interest in the outdoors is growing, so too are the threats to our National Parks. The book should help to impress on outdoor lovers that access such as we have was not easily attained. It should help in making us more vigilant, and determined to oppose any threat to the countryside from whatever source it might come.

If this book helps in doing this, my efforts in its preparation will have been well worth while.

Benny Rothman
Timperley 1982

Kinder Reservoir

"The Manchester Rambler"

ve been over Snowdon, I've slept upon Crowden,
ve camped by the Wain Stores as well,
ve sun-bathed on Kinder, been burned to a cinder,
nd many more things I can tell.
y rucksack has oft been my pillow,
he heather has oft been my bed,
nd sooner than part from the mountains,
think I would rather be dead.

HORUS

m a rambler, I'm a rambler from Manchester way,
get all my pleasure the hard, moorland way,
may be a wage slave on Monday,
ut I am a free man on Sunday.

There's pleasure in dragging through peat bogs
    and bragging
Of all the fine walks that you know;
There's even a measure of some kind of pleasure
In wading through ten feet of snow.
I've stood on the edge of the Downfall,
And seen all the valleys outspread,
And sooner than part from the mountains,
I think I would rather be dead. (Cho.)

The day was just ending as I was descending
Through Grindsbrook just by Upper-Tor,
When a voice cried, "Hey, you!", in the way
    keepers do,
(He'd the worst face that ever I saw).
The things that he said were unpleasant;
In the teeth of his fury I said
That sooner than part from the mountains,
I think I would rather be dead. (Cho.)

He called me a louse and said "Think of the
    grouse".
Well, I thought but I still couldn't see
Why old Kinder Scout and the moors round about
Couldn't take both the poor grouse and me.
He said, "All this land is my master's".
At that I stood shaking my head,
No man has the right to own mountains
Any more than the deep ocean bed. (Cho.)

I once loved a maid, a spot-welder by trade,
She was fair as the rowan in bloom,
And the blue of her eye matched the June
    moorland sky,
And I loved her from April to June.
On the day that we should have been married,
I went for a ramble instead,
For sooner than part from the mountains,
I think I would rather be dead. (Cho.)

So I'll walk where I will over mountain and hill
And I'll lie where the bracken is deep,
I belong to the mountains, the clear running
    fountains
Where the grey rocks rise rugged and steep.
I have seen the white hare in the gulleys,
And the curlew fly high overhead,
And sooner than part from the mountains
I think I would rather be dead. (Cho.)

Words and Music by Ewan MacColl— press officer on the Kinder Trespass.

9

CHAPTER ONE
Living for the Weekends

They scrambled up the steep bank off William Clough and on to Kinder Scout. Hundreds of ramblers on the Mass Trespass shook hands and congratulated each other. They had overcome their first hurdle. They were standing on forbidden land, tantalizing glimpses of which they had seen from time to time in their rambles along the well-trodden paths around Kinder.

Today, anybody with a good pair of legs and lungs, and the will to do so, can go on to Kinder at most times of the year, apart from a few days during the Shooting Season, and on rare occasions when drought conditions and fire risks cause the moorland to be closed. In 1932 this was not possible. The fifteen square miles of Kinder, although encircled by paths, was not crossed by a single public footpath. Kinder itself contained spots of outstanding interest and rugged beauty and was a challenge to every rambler.

It is not remarkable that the Mass Trespass of 1932 happened. The trespassers were attacking the injustice of the Enclosure Acts, imposed on the public a century earlier, which confiscated common land and handed it in parcels to landowners. At the time of the original enclosures the landowners' main interest was sheep rearing; today, as in 1932, it is the business of grouse shooting, the sport of a tiny section of wealthy people.

1932 was a grim year in Britain. Unemployment had reached peak proportions and particularly hard hit were the big industrial areas of Lancashire and Yorkshire. Manchester, Salford, Sheffield and the dozens of smaller towns and villages in the counties were deserts of bricks, mortar and cobblestones. Living conditions were desperately bad with bug-ridden and verminous houses. Not many had gardens, there were very few trees, shrubs or flowers in the soul-destroying waste. The only way to enjoy a little fresh air and sunshine was to escape to the countryside. Even though public parks existed in towns, these were no substitute for the real thing.

Opposite: Kinder Low from Mermaid's Pool.

11

Rambling and cycling were mass sports. Cars were too expensive for most people. The railway companies competed for the custom of ramblers. Rambling clubs and federations and associations together with railway companies organised special rail tickets for walkers. Tea-rooms and cheap cafes catered for the thousands of ramblers and cyclists who poured into the countryside every weekend. Most newspapers of the period had a rambling column. Special rambles led by experienced walkers were regularly advertised in local newspapers and ramblers' excursions were put on by railway companies from time to time. Rambling and cycling had come of age. Town dwellers lived for weekends when they could go camping in the country, while unemployed young people would return home just to 'sign on' at the Labour Exchanges and collect their dole money. Rambling, cycling and camping clubs grew in membership.

A feature of Sunday mornings was the cycling clubs strung out along the country lanes and roads. Cycling club houses were packed on Sunday evenings when clubs met after their day's outing for a sing-song and dance – not only young bloods on racing bikes, but husbands and wives on tandems, and grandads and grandmas riding their light-weight bikes. The Sunday morning queues of ramblers on London Road (Piccadilly) Station stretched down the station approaches. The platforms rang to the sound of nailed boots: rubber and Vibram soles had not yet been invented. Most working class ramblers wore ex-army boots which they nailed themselves, and often they wore them at work to break them in. Rambling gear was very varied, shorts were usually worn by both the lads and girls, together with coloured shirts, sweaters and often ex-army jackets. More sober knee-breeches and woollen jackets were reserved for 'posh' rambling clubs. Anoraks were unknown in Britain.

Camping too was more free and easy and rough and ready. The regulations on camping, restricting it to licensed sites only, had not yet come into existence. Tents were only of the bivouac type. The sophisticated canvas homes now so popular were not then available. Camp fires, dixies and primus stoves were the only way to cook meals, but despite the apparent inconvenience compared with today's standards, weekends in the country made life worth living.

Weekend and holiday camps in the country grew year by year both in numbers and in popularity. Young people were escaping from the squalor and monotony of the towns on bikes and on foot, but as the numbers of cyclists and ramblers grew new problems

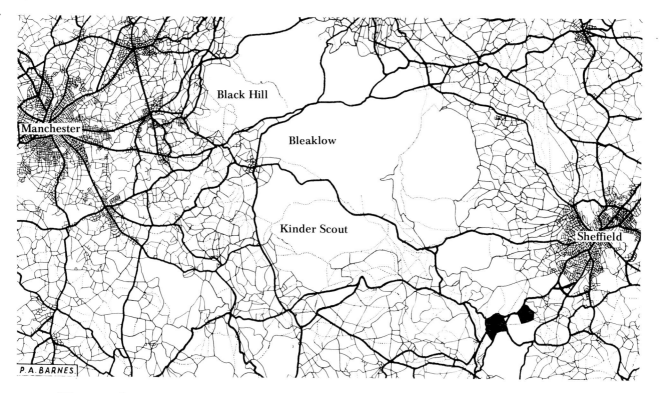

P.A.BARNES.

arose. The popular footpaths of the Peak District soon became morasses and quagmires in wet weather. The feeling of being close to nature receded as the crowds grew, and ramblers looked longingly at the acres of empty peat bogs, moorlands and the tops, which were forbidden territory.

They were not just forbidden, they were guarded by gamekeepers armed with sticks, which some were not afraid to use against solitary walkers. The more adventurous ramblers, when and where they could, would break off the footpaths onto the private land, but the wily gamekeepers watching through telescopes from hiding places would try to head them off. Some of the more unreasonable keepers, instead of escorting ramblers to the nearest footpath, would force them to walk miles out of their way, causing them to miss their train connections. Very often a keeper would provoke a scuffle with a rambler who would be given a beating, but there were occasions when the rambler, instead of being at the receiving end of a beating would administer one to the keeper. All the forces of law and order would be brought into use to track down any rambler who hit back before he even reached a railway station, and that part of the country would be denied him for ever more, if he were caught.

Above: The roads and footpaths between Manchester and Sheffield in 1934 showing the extremely limited access to the wide belt of moorland between the two cities.

13

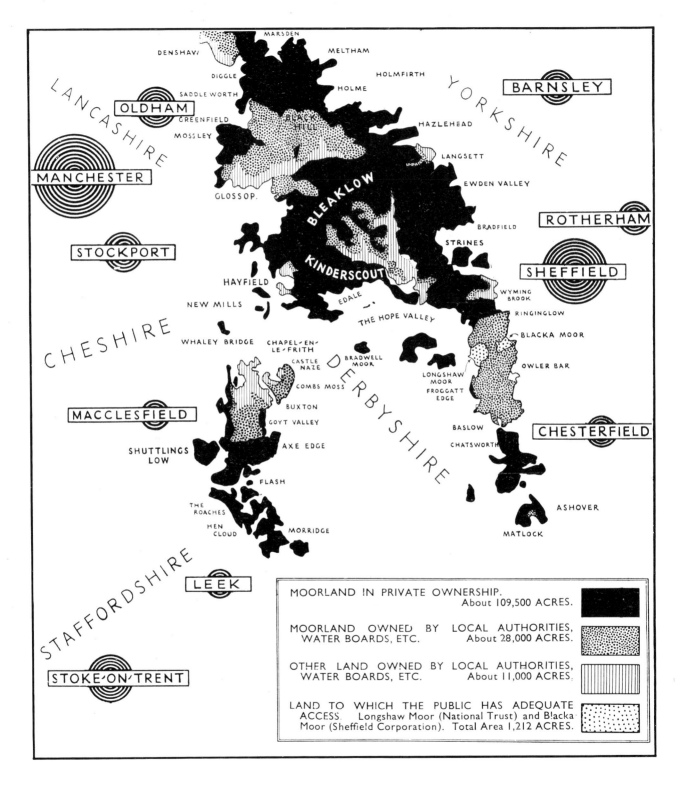

MARSDEN

DENSHAW

DIGGLE

MELTHAM

HOLMFIRTH

SADDLEWORTH

HOLME

OLDHAM

GREENFIELD

BLACK HILL

HAZLEHEAD

MOSSLEY

BARNSLEY

MANCHESTER

LANGSETT

EWDEN VALLEY

GLOSSOP.

BLEAKLOW

BRADFIELD

ROTHERHAM

STRINES

STOCKPORT

KINDERSCOUT

SHEFFIELD

HAYFIELD

WYMING BROOK

NEW MILLS

EDALE

RINGINGLOW

THE HOPE VALLEY

BLACKA MOOR

WHALEY BRIDGE

CHAPEL-EN-LE-FRITH

BRADWELL MOOR

OWLER BAR

CHESHIRE

CASTLE NAZE

LONGSHAW MOOR

DERBYSHIRE

COMBS MOSS

FROGGATT EDGE

BUXTON

MACCLESFIELD

GOYT VALLEY

BASLOW

CHESTERFIELD

SHUTTLINGS LOW

AXE EDGE

CHATSWORTH

FLASH

THE ROACHES

ASHOVER

HEN CLOUD

MORRIDGE

MATLOCK

LANCASHIRE

STAFFORDSHIRE

LEEK

STOKE-ON-TRENT

YORKSHIRE

MOORLAND IN PRIVATE OWNERSHIP.
About 109,500 ACRES.

MOORLAND OWNED BY LOCAL AUTHORITIES, WATER BOARDS, ETC. About 28,000 ACRES.

OTHER LAND OWNED BY LOCAL AUTHORITIES, WATER BOARDS, ETC. About 11,000 ACRES.

LAND TO WHICH THE PUBLIC HAS ADEQUATE ACCESS. Longshaw Moor (National Trust) and Blacka Moor (Sheffield Corporation). Total Area 1,212 ACRES.

14

In theory it was possible to obtain permission from landowners to ramble on moorland. In practice it was very difficult. The duplicated letter (right) to a rambler, Mr. Colley, from Mr. Watts, an owner of Kinder Scout, is a typical example. As more town dwellers flocked from the towns into the countryside the bitterness and frustration grew.

Since 1884 attempts had been made for an 'Access to Mountains' Bill to be presented in Parliament to give the Public the unrestricted right to walk on uncultivated moorland. The hopes of such an Act being passed seemed to recede as the years passed by. Some Members of Parliament (often prominent Members) expressed their sympathy and support. Liberal newspapers railed at the injustice of the situation, mass demonstrations of ramblers were held, but the might of the land-owning lobby was too powerful. By 1932 the 'Access to Mountains' Act was as far away as ever. It was in this situation that the British Workers' Sports Federation began to organise open air activity in the North.

Previously, the Federation had been mainly London-based. It was started in 1928 essentially as a working-class movement to organise sport for workers.

In London the B.W.S.F. had successfully run Sunday football leagues at a time when there was no organised football on a Sunday, as it was expressly forbidden by many amateur football associations. In some parts of London it had successfully campaigned for dressing room facilities and football pitches, particularly in some of the deprived areas like Stepney and Tottenham. The B.W.S.F. was accepted as a leader in this field. In the Manchester area it held its first camp at Easter 1930 in Disley. From then on it organised weekend Easter and Whitweek camps in Marple, Rowarth and Little Hayfield, so introducing many young people to the countryside. Inevitably, the favourite events were the organised rambles, and it was arising from such a ramble at our Rowarth camp at Easter 1932 that the idea of the Mass Trespass originated.

The ramblers had intended to go on to Bleaklow, but the small band was stopped at Yellow Slacks by a group of gamekeepers. They were abused, threatened and turned back. To add to the humiliation of the Manchester ramblers, a number of those present were from the London B.W.S.F. on a visit to the Peak District, and they were astounded by the incident. There were not enough ramblers to force their way through, so, crestfallen, they had to return to camp without the Londoners seeing the wildness

S. & J. WATTS & Cᵒ

JAMES WATTS
HUMPHREY WATTS
HENRY LIONEL WATTS
JAMES WATTS JUN.

MANCHESTER.

Telegraphic Address "WATTSES"

It has been my practice of late to allow members of the public, who asked for such permission, to walk over my portion of Kinder Scout, when I could do so without detriment to the value of the ground as a grouse moor.

Applications have, however, become so numerous, that as a result of trying to give permission as much as possible, the Downfall area is now completely deserted by grouse, which will not stay on ground which is continually disturbed.

As I am still taxed and rated on the sporting value of this ground as if it still existed, I trust that those who apply will not think me unreasonable if I am compelled to refuse permission and try to recreate the value on which I am made to pay.

JAMES WATTS.

Opposite: 1934 map indicating the comparatively small areas of land open to the public.

of Bleaklow with its groughs and peatbogs. Back at camp, it was agreed that if enough ramblers had been there, no body of keepers could have kept them off the moorland. We decided to organise a Mass Trespass to prove our point.

After the camp, the Manchester area committee of The British Workers' Sports Federation, with representatives from Manchester, Eccles, Salford, Swinton and Stockport, met and decided on a Mass Trespass on to Kinder Scout. Why Kinder Scout? Because this was the outstanding stretch of moorland uncrossed by even a single footpath; its rugged tops could be seen from many points on the public footpaths and roads around, and it was the forbidden territory most known to the hundreds of ramblers travelling from Hayfield, Glossop, Chinley and Edale.

BWSF Camp at Rowarth

Right: Seal Edge, Kinder (Top) Kinder Downfall — banned to ramblers in 1932.

PEAK TRESPASS PROTESTS.

MOB LAW ON THE MOORS.

DAMAGING EFFECT OF "MASS TRESPASS."

RAMBLERS OBJECT TO DRASTIC MOVE.

Much of the sympathy and influence which have been enlisted in support of the Access to Mountains Bill, which, it is hoped, will eventually become law, is likely the "Evening Chronicle" is able to state, to be alienated if the proposal of a Manchester rambling organisation to organise a "mass trespass" on Kinder Scout on Sunday is persisted in.

This method of enforcing claims "for free access to beauty spots" has been devised by the Lancashire district of the British Workers' Sports Federation, but it commands no support from the scores of other rambling organisations which exist in the Manchester district.

The danger of "mob law" usurping constitutional methods in the ventilation of grievances, real or imagined, is viewed with apprehension not only by landowners, but by thousands of ramblers.

PRIVILEGES APPRECIATED.

It is pointed out that the general body of ramblers are keenly appreciative of the privileges they enjoy by the good grace of landowners in the Peak District, and the prospect of facing a brush with the police in the attempt to enforce a claim, which

would at best be of doubtful benefit, is abhorrent to most of them.

The view is generally held that trespass on land which costs considerable sums to maintain, and which provides employment for a considerable number of people, is indefensible.

DOING NO SERVICE.

"Those who trespass, however well-meaning they may be, will do the rambling movement no service," said a well-known Manchester rambling official to the Evening Chronicle to-day.

"There are many paths which are open to all ramblers, and practically all the best country is crossed by such public paths. In cases where paths are wrongfully closed the Footpaths Society takes the matter up.

"But where there are no such paths ramblers are better advised if they apply to the proprietors for permission before walking over the land.

"Those who organise these trespasses should take care that they do not allow themselves to be confused with hooligan elements who do wilful damage.

"They would be wiser to devote their energies to supporting the movement of the Ramblers' Federation and other open-air bodies in favour of the Access to Mountains Bill, the object of which is to secure the same rights for ramblers, but by legal means."

Kinder, he added, was particularly unsuitable for such activity, in view of the danger to ramblers who became detached from the main body.

The Manchester Evening Chronicle venting its fears during the week before the Trespass.

CHAPTER TWO
Opposition

The decision to organize a Mass Trespass was taken, and publicity for the event started immediately. As the secretary of the Lancashire B.W.S.F., I visited the Manchester Evening Chronicle and gave an interview on the proposed Trespass. The paper prominently published the interview, embellishing it by saying that the B.W.S.F. was proposing to throw hundreds of 'shock troops' on to Kinder. (This was in 1932 before Hitler's shock troops had even been heard of outside Germany.)

The reaction in the rambling world was instantaneous. The Manchester Ramblers' Federation was hostile to the Trespass. Prominent ramblers' leaders prophesied dire consequences if the Mass Trespass took place, one saying that it would put back access to mountains by forty years and antagonise the landowners, but in Sheffield, where the rambling movement was at a more grass roots level, they were not so antagonistic. Most newspapers were hostile and letters of opposition appeared in the correspondence columns during the following week. In addition we published duplicated leaflets and handed them out to ramblers at the station during the weekend prior to the Trespass. These were generally well received.

We announced a ramblers' meeting at the Hayfield recreation ground for Sunday, April 24th, commencing at 2 pm, followed by a Mass Trespass over Kinder Scout. We decided on a speaker, I was to act as chairman, and we appointed stewards for both the meeting and the Trespass. We did not announce or even plan the route: that was to be decided on the day. This was not a clever tactic on our part, it was sheer inexperience. However, we were fully convinced of the justice of our cause and felt that this was sufficient to ensure success. For the next few days the arguments for and against the Mass Trespass raged in the newspaper columns.

DIRECT ACTION BY RAMBLERS.

"MASS TRESPASS" ON KINDER SCOUT

TO ENFORCE ACCESS CLAIMS.

Three hundred ramblers belonging to working-class organisations will advance on Kinder Scout, Derbyshire, on Sunday next to enforce their claims for free access to the beauty spots of the countryside.

This method of mass trespasses on disputed territory has been devised by the Lancashire district of the British Workers' Sports Federation, who are asking all clubs affiliated with them to meet at Hayfield on Sunday, from which spot the advance will be made.

The ramblers state they are "tired of unproductive protests and pleas" and they hope by this new method to force landowners to concede them the right to ramble over their property.

There is no public footpath over Kinder, a fact which the ramblers regard as an injustice.

PROTESTS INEFFECTIVE.

"We are pinning our faith in this method," Mr. B. Rothman, secretary of the Lancashire district of the British Workers' Sports Federation stated to-day.

"All of the fifteen clubs in Lancashire affiliated to our organisation will be represented at the rally, and they will be augmented by two of our Sheffield clubs.

"With sufficient support we believe we can make our action effective, even in face of the opposition we shall no doubt receive from gamekeepers and police.

"We feel we cannot any longer submit to being deprived of the beauties of the countryside for the convenience of the landowners.

"Wherever we claim we have a just right to go we shall trespass en masse. And Sunday will be but the opening our our campaign."

One of our problems was that the B.W.S.F. was not an integral part of the Ramblers' Federation. We were newcomers to rambling. In addition, we were essentially a working class movement and most of the established rambling clubs consisted of either middle-class professional people, or specialist ramblers such as ornithologists, botanists and geologists. They were highly suspicious of us, and we were frankly suspicious of them. They believed that we were 'politically motivated' (to use a modern term), and loutish. We knew that many of the more exclusive clubs were occasionally obtaining permits to go on to the moorland, and were also beginning to go abroad where access problems did not arise. We doubted that they wanted us on the moors any more than did the landowners, and they appeared to be quite happy with the existing state of affairs.

To add to the problems there was a very big age gap between us. We were very young, almost entirely under twenty-one years of age. The established rambling clubs were of a far older age group, many of whose members were middle aged and had spent a lifetime in the rambling movement. We were impatient at the seemingly futile efforts so far made to achieve access to mountains. Conditions in towns were becoming more intolerable and unemployment, which stood at about 4 million, greatly added to our frustration. We believed that we could achieve a breakthrough, and went full steam ahead. The patronising opposition of many rambling organisation leaders, and the downright hostility of the landowners' lobby, only strengthened our determination.

Opposite: Press and ramblers' organizations reactions to the publicized Trespass.

Below: Invitation to people in Eccles to take part in the Mass Trespass.

B. W. S. F.
RAMBLER'S RALLY.

The Rally will take place on Sunday April 24th. at 2 o-clock on Hayfield Recreation Ground. From the Rec. we proceed on a MASS TRESPASS onto Kinder Scout. This is being organised by the British Workers Sports Federation, who fight for Ramblers:-

"Against the finest stretches of Moorlands being closed to us.
"For Cheap fares. Forcheap catering facilities.
"Against any war preparations in rambling organisations.
"Against petty restrictions such as singing etc.

Now: young workers of Eccles, to all, whether you've been rambling before or not, we extend a hearty welcome.

If you've not been rambling before, start now, you don't know what you've missed. Roll up at Eccles at 8-15. on Sunday Morning. and come with us for the best day out that you have ever had.

FARE 1/6 Return.   TEA 8d extra,   Eccles Cross 8-15 a.m.

On Trespassing.

As an inveterate trespasser, the idea of a "mass trespass" on Kinder Scout, which, I see, is planned for Sunday, does not appeal to me.

That may sound odd, but I always think the essence of trespassing is that it should be done quietly, neatly, and successfully.

Trespassing is done best alone, or with one or at the most two companions. When you do it with a crowd all the fun goes out of it. And there is fun in it—a sort of adult substitute for the pleasure which every youngster gets in raiding an orchard.

Making the Most of It.

If you get away with it you have done no harm (or at least I hope you haven't), and if you don't escape detection you may achieve even more.

The tactful trespasser who is stopped by farmers or gamekeepers (the latter are usually more difficult to manage) can very often make a friend for life.

I have met one or two of the pleasantest people I know while trespassing on their land. I will not attempt to explain how it is done. Everything depends on realising what sort of a man you are dealing with and your own skill. If you have enough of it, you may be asked to come again and so win rights of way and privileges that can never be secured by Act of Parliament or public demonstrations.

Ramblers Speak Out.

To THE EDITOR OF THE EVENING CHRONICLE

SIR,—In view of the publicity which has been given to the proposed mass trespass on Kinder on Sunday next, we wish to record our protest against such a method, which we consider can only ultimately prejudice the objects which the orderly rambler has at heart.

We wish also to state that the Ramblers' Federation (Manchester and District) have no connection with the organisation which proposes this trespass.—N. WILLINGTON, General Secretary.

Ramblers' Ways.

THE Lancashire ramblers who have planned a "mass trespass" in Derbyshire next Sunday surely overstate their case when they declare they cannot submit to being "deprived of the beauties of the countryside for the convenience of landowners." "Trespassers will be prosecuted" is still far too common a notice in this country, but most of the districts worth the tramper's attention are fairly well supplied with footpaths—even if some of them are metaphorically hedged by conditions.

CERTAINLY legislation to help the rambler and country-lover moves slowly in this country—how many years is it since the Access to Mountains Bill was first thought of?—and the filching of public footpaths still goes on. But ramblers must remember that "mass trespass" is a two-edged sword and one that is more likely to provoke the withdrawal of privileges granted by private owners than to extend them.

AT present ramblers have the sympathy of the public in their efforts to win more facilities. We would not like to see them risk losing that support by unnecessarily provoking measures. There are sufficient ramblers in this country to make Parliament listen to them if they will organise themselves properly. A determined badgering of M.P.s on the lines recently adopted by the opponents of the Sunday Cinemas Bill would work wonders.

CHAPTER THREE
The Trespass

Sunday, 24th April, dawned clear and bright. Early in the morning I was off to Hayfield with my friend and colleague, Woolfie Winnick. We went on our bikes, as, in addition to being ramblers, both of us were keen cyclists. This was fortunate because, as I was to learn later, the police had obtained an injunction to restrain me from going on the Trespass, and had spent a fruitless week trying to serve it on me. Apparently, whenever they called at my home I was out and nobody could inform them of my whereabouts. On the morning of 24th April they were on watch at London Road Station to serve the injunction on me. Fortunately for me, and unfortunately for the police, I never went near the station. It is hard to speculate what would have happened if they had served me with the injunction. It would obviously have created additional problems, and might have diverted us from our main objective.

En route to Hayfield, Woolfie and I discussed possible routes on to Kinder, and alternative venues for our meeting if Hayfield recreation ground should prove unsuitable. When we reached Hayfield we went to a tea-room, had a drink of tea and stored away our bikes and then went to survey the intended Trespass. We spent about two and a half to three hours looking at possible routes. On the tops we could see clusters of gamekeepers lurking on the look-out, and after finally deciding that William Clough – Sandy Heys – Kinder was our best bet, we returned to Hayfield. On our way back we passed a number of possible sites for our meeting. One was a flat space at the end of Valley Road, and another a disused quarry close by. The quarry was the most convenient as a projecting rock formed a platform overlooking a natural amphitheatre below. It was well sited as it would give the ramblers a break before the William Clough section and time to organise and prepare for the possible struggle ahead.

It must have been about one o'clock when we got back to Hayfield and the picture had completely changed. From a quiet deserted

Opposite & Below: Hayfield

village it had become a packed centre of activity. Police were everywhere. We learned later that one third of the Derbyshire Police Force under the personal command of the Derbyshire Deputy Chief Constable, was concentrated in and around the village, and some were stationed in a local cinema. The recreation ground was full of ramblers, and still more were coming from the tea-rooms and cafes, having arrived earlier and refreshed themselves for the battles ahead. Woolfie and I melted into the crowd, to meet our mates. Again it was very fortunate for me. I learned later that the police had been on watch at Hayfield Station to serve me with their injunction, and were even on the look-out for me at the recreation ground.

We gathered a small group of our committee together. It was obvious that it would be very easy for the police to trap the crowd in the recreation ground. This was at a lower level than the surrounding roads and exits could easily be blocked. We did not know what the police intentions were, but we were not prepared to take any chances of the day's events finishing up at the recreation ground before the walk had even started, so we decided to move off before the appointed time of 2 pm. We learned later in evidence given by Council officials that meetings were not permitted in the recreation ground. We sent our colleagues through the crowd and into the adjoining cafes telling ramblers to move quietly into Valley Road, a small road very difficult for motor traffic (police cars) and started to walk in the direction of William Clough.

Soon a small army of ramblers was on the march, estimated by the press at about four hundred. The police were caught on the hop. They could not get in front of the ramblers to stop us (short of fighting their way through our ranks) nor could they use their vehicles because of the nature of the road, and as they could not predict which way we would turn when we reached the end of the road, it was impossible for them to head us off. So they fell in ignominiously behind the ramblers. I have heard transcripts of reports from police officers who were there on the day which confirm this. On we marched, cheerfully singing and talking, until we reached the first alternative meeting site. We stopped to hold our meeting but were immediately approached by Stockport waterworks' officials who warned us that meetings on their property were prohibited (it was apparently their ground). We did not want a battle with the Stockport Water Authority on this issue. Our objective was Kinder Scout, so we moved off to the quarry site. This was by far the better site from every point of view, both acoustically and strategically. I scrambled onto the natural pulpit and started to address the crowd below.

Above: One of the waterworks officials who warned off the Trespassers, talking to Benny Rothman in the BBC 'Look Stranger' programme on the Trespass in July 1970.

Left: The march towards Kinder after the meeting in the quarry.

Overleaf: Benny Rothman addressing the crowd at the quarry. Standing behind is one of the members of the organising committee Lance Helman.

Above: The author surveys the scene in the quarry, April 1981.

Top: A section of the crowd at the quarry meeting. The men seen near the back wearing hats were water board officials and detectives.

It was an inspiring picture. There were hundreds of young men and women, lads and girls, in their picturesque rambling gear: shorts of every length and colour, flannels and breeches, even overalls, vivid colours and drab khaki, (khaki shorts and shirts were fashionable at the time), multi-coloured sweaters and pullovers, army packs and rucksacks of every size and shape. (It was the 'done thing' at that time to carry enormous rucksacks crammed to capacity.)

Without any preliminaries I started to speak. Originally it had been intended that I would be chairman and that Jack, one of the older members, would address the meeting. He was a big, fine, strapping chap, a very good speaker with an excellent knowledge of the history of the fight for 'Access to Mountains', but unfortunately he was unable to do this on the day. I have forgotten the exact reasons, but as there was not time to find a replacement I had to fill the gap. It did not really matter because I had a most sympathetic audience. They laughed at any semblance of a joke, and when I had finished they gave me a tremendous round of applause. I very briefly outlined the history of the injustice of enclosures, which had stolen Common Land from the people in a fraudulent series of so-called Enclosure Acts. I sketched the history of the 'Access to Mountains' agitation from its inception in 1884, nearly fifty years earlier, and the ruthless landowners' lobby which had frustrated any effort to pass the Bill through Parliament.

I instanced the success of the B.W.S.F. in securing better football facilities in London, through mass activities, and called for the Mass Trespass as a start to a campaign to back-up the other organisations fighting for 'Access to Mountains'. I denied the stories in the media that said we were hooligans intent on trouble. We were not intending to injure or damage anybody or anything. We wanted a peaceful demonstration ramble, but were determined not to be diverted or stopped.

I gave instructions on the 'whistle signals' we would use to control the ramble – one blast for stop, two for turn right, three for advance in open formation – then amid tremendous applause from the walkers I scrambled off the speaker's rock and into the crowd. As I did so, Woolfie Winnick blew the whistle for the start of the ramble and was leading the walkers along the road towards William Clough.

As I reached the crowd, a small group of B.W.S.F. ramblers surrounded me acting as an informal bodyguard. This was not arranged nor agreed to, it just happened. They were determined that there should be no arrests, and none was made as we started the second leg of our demonstration.

Overleaf: Trespassers posing for photographs before the climb up the path past Kinder Reservoir.

Along the road towards Kinder Reservoir we marched, cheerful and jubilant, with the sweating and panting police in the rear. At the meeting the police had adopted a low profile, keeping to the fringes of the crowd. Now they re-grouped at the rear of the ramblers. As we went through gates, over brooks and stiles, the front sections of the ramblers waited until the whole group emerged, then carried on. This prevented any arrests along the route. Again, this was not pre-arranged, but happened spontaneously on the day. Up the steep bank on to White Brow we scrambled, admiring the Kinder Reservoir below, and then on to Nab Brow and the William Clough footpath. The whole of the body of ramblers was now well into William Clough. At the point agreed earlier between Woolfie and myself, roughly about one-third to a half of the distance to Ashop Head, Woolfie, who was leading the ramble, blew his whistle for a right turn. Our stewards in the body of the ramblers turned right, then the crowd of ramblers commenced a slow scramble up the face towards the top of Kinder Scout in a long 'open formation' line. This was to ensure that if any section was stopped, the rest would still be able to carry on and achieve the objective.

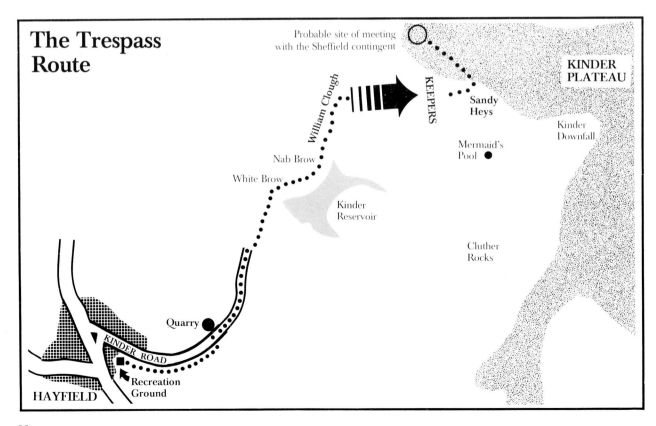

The Trespass Route

About half-way up the scramble groups of gamekeepers emerged shouting to the ramblers to stop, and threatening them with their sticks. There were probably only three or four groups of keepers along the whole line, about twenty to thirty men in all. One temporary keeper, Edward Beever, became involved in a scuffle in which he was hurt, though not seriously, as he was able to walk back to Hayfield after the incident. Most keepers brandished their sticks and threatened to use them if the ramblers did not turn back, but wisely did nothing but bluster as the ramblers pushed them aside and carried on. One or two, however, did use their sticks on ramblers, and were promptly disarmed. Woolfie Winnick was struck on the head by a keeper. Unfortunately for the keeper, Woolfie was, amongst other things, a competent amateur boxer, and a very much wiser keeper nursed a painful jaw after the event. As the long line of ramblers scrambled uphill, one group came upon a nest with a bird sitting on its eggs. They promptly put a picket on the nest to make sure that the bird was not disturbed. I encountered no keepers on my section of the front.

Above:Edward Beever receiving first aid.

Opposite: Keepers using their sticks on one of the protesters. (Inset) Some of the keepers on the ridge top in a scene from the 'Look Stranger' programme.

As we approached the top of the scramble another big group was seen on the skyline. For a moment or two we braced ourselves for a major encounter, and were very relieved when we were greeted by an enthusiastic group of our own supporters from Sheffield who had come via Edale, and late-comers from the Manchester area who had come by other routes. We learned from them that every railway station en route was teeming with police and that there were police patrols on the roads. We exchanged congratulations and experiences, and decided to hold a victory meeting.

The moor where the confrontation took place.

I addressed the crowd again, together with a Sheffield rambler, and on this occasion Jack Clayton of the Manchester B.W.S.F. committee also spoke, emphasising that only people familiar with Kinder should make their way back in a group separate from the main body; we did not want any of our party to be lost on Kinder. We were on the holy of holies, the forbidden territory of Kinder Scout. So far there had been no arrests and no direct police interference, but we wondered whether this position would change before the end of the day.

We decided to go back as we had come, one strong, united body, and not disperse in all directions like a band of criminals. It was by no means a schoolboy prank with everybody trying to pretend they had not been involved. It was a demonstration for the rights of ordinary people to walk on land stolen from them in earlier times; we were proud of our effort and proudly marched back the way we had come, the Manchester group to Hayfield and the Sheffield group to Edale. We were not afraid of standing up and being counted for our beliefs.

CHAPTER FOUR
Arrest and Trial

The police who had not faced the scramble uphill on to Kinder, had returned to Hayfield for further re-grouping and fresh orders. They were instructed to make some arrests, consequently when we returned to Hayfield we were faced with a strong force of police stretched across Kinder Road, which brought us to a halt.

We stopped the ramblers and waited. It would have been counter productive to try to break through and start a battle with the police. We had achieved our objective, the next move was with the establishment.

Some policemen accompanied by keepers moved across the ranks of the ramblers and made five arrests. There was no attempt on our part to resist, nor was there any effort made to rescue any of those arrested. I was among those taken to Hayfield Lock-up for interrogation and to be charged. When we arrived at the Lock-up we found that another rambler had previously been arrested at the scene of the scuffle with the injured special keeper. He, it seems, was one of the few ramblers opposed to the Mass Trespass. He had gone along, following in the rear of the ramblers. On seeing the scuffle and the keeper on the ground he claims he went forward to assist him. He was an easy target, being on his own, so the police promptly arrested him and took him back to Hayfield at the time when the main body of ramblers was either still scrambling on to Kinder Scout, or on Kinder at the meeting with our Sheffield Group.

Inside the Lock-up we had our names taken. There was great excitement among the police when I gave my name, as they had been on the look-out for me all day to serve me with the injunction. I do not know what description of me had been given, or how they had proposed to identify me. In evidence at the various court hearings, both at New Mills and at Derby, the police witnesses claimed to have arrested me because they recognised me as the speaker at the quarry, but they certainly did not know that the speaker at the quarry was the man for whom they had been searching during the preceding week. The ramblers arrested were John Anderson aged 21, arrested at the scene of the scuffle with a temporary keeper; Jud Clynes, aged 23; Harry Mendel, aged 23; David Nussbaum, aged 19; Arthur Gillett, aged 19; and myself, Bernard Rothman, aged 20.

Meanwhile outside, a big body of ramblers waited for us to be released. When about an hour or so had elapsed and we were still being kept in custody, they elected 9 spokesmen, hammered on the door, offered bail on our behalf, and pressed for our release. The situation was beginning to look ugly, so the police smuggled us out through a rear door and took us to New Mills Police Station.

We were kept overnight at New Mills. With hindsight, I now realise that we should have challenged this at the time. The year was 1932, the telephone had been invented, and the excuse of establishing our identities, before we could be released, was very thin indeed. Verification could have been made in an hour or two at the most.

The real reason was, of course, that the establishment had been very badly hurt by the event, and could not decide with what we were to be charged. They wanted time to decide on the most serious charges possible, and also to intimidate us, and ramblers in general.

The next day when we appeared at New Mills Police Court we were all charged with unlawful assembly and breach of the peace, and were remanded on bail until May 11th. John Anderson was also charged with causing grievous bodily harm to Edward Beever, temporary keeper, and similarly remanded on that charge.

We duly appeared at the New Mills' Court on 11th May. On the first day of the trial the charges were read out. John Anderson's case was to be considered at a Special Hearing later.

It is significant that no charges of trespass or damage were brought against anybody in spite of the fact that this was the reason for all the events. We were all first offenders; none of us had ever before been in a court. Arthur (Tony) Gillett, who came from a wealthy banking family, was represented in court, as were John Anderson, Jud Clynes, Dave Nussbaum and Harry Mendel; I conducted my own defence. This had been decided upon by the B.W.S.F. Committee as it was thought that no solicitor was likely to conduct

The reference to 'Lord Big Bug' was taken from a book by Lord Baden Powell and was used on a poster found on a door in Hayfield. The advertisement inviting people to join the Trespass included the question: "Is it a crime for workers to put their feet where Lord Big Bug and Lady Flea do their annual shooting?"

SEQUEL TO HIKERS' PROTEST

CHARGES FOLLOW ALLEGED TRESPASS

LORD BIG BUG

NOTICES POSTED ON A DOOR

From Our Special Correspondent

NEW MILLS, Wednesday.

SIX young men were accused at the police court here to-day with offences alleged to have been committed during the mass trespass on Kinder Scout on April 24.

the defence on the basis of history and politics.

We were later criticised by some leaders of the rambling movement for not engaging an outstanding barrister, but at the time they neither offered us any help, nor suggested that we do this.

The police brought a considerable number of detectives of all ranks and police constables as witnesses, in addition to keepers, and employees of Hayfield Council and Stockport Waterworks. Not a single private citizen from the district was produced by the prosecution to justify their claim that the proposed Mass Trespass had caused fear or apprehension in the minds of people in the district. The Court then adjourned and resumed the next day. On this occasion, only Gillett was legally represented. The defence brought no witnesses. The cost of travel, and the loss of wages it would have involved, deterred any witnesses from coming forward on our behalf.

The prosecution witnesses were questioned by the defence solicitors and by myself, and finally I made a defence submission which was carefully taken down in longhand by the Clerk of the Court. He was outraged at the length of the statement, and constantly interrupted me, but I carried on until I had finished what I had to say. This took about seventy-five minutes, to the great indignation of the prosecution.

Above: Three of the "Trespassers" in the BBC 'Look Stranger' programme (left) the author (middle) the late Dave Nesbitt (right) Tony Gillett.

To summarise my statement: it dealt with the unhappy state of affairs in town and cities for young people, and their desire for the open country; the over-crowding and unsatisfactory state of footpaths at peak periods at weekends and holiday times; and the injustice of the filching of the Derbyshire moorlands for grouse shooting. It put forward the belief of the B.W.S.F. in the need for mass action by ramblers if access to mountains was to be achieved. It pointed to examples of successes achieved in the past by ramblers in saving footpaths, and by sportsmen in obtaining sports facilities through mass protests. It then analysed the prosecution evidence, pointing to contradictory statements made by police and other witnesses. It finally dealt with the scuffles which ensued, and refuted any suggestion of hooliganism or incited violence on the part of the ramblers, pointing out that the only violence which occurred came from stick-wielding keepers.

The submission concluded: 'The demonstration of April 24th was a peaceful demonstration to gain support for our contention of the right of access to mountains. The assembly at the quarry, if that is the assembly which is alleged to be an unlawful assembly, gave no-one any reason to fear a breach of the peace. If this is correct I simply plead not guilty to the charge'. All my colleagues also pleaded 'not guilty'. The Court decided to commit all the ramblers to the Derby Assizes which opened on June 29th.

The special hearing against John Anderson took place a week later in New Mills and he was remanded to Derby Assizes on the charge of causing grievous bodily harm to special keeper Edward Beever, in addition to the other charges made against the rest of us. When John Anderson appeared he was not represented by a solicitor, nor were any witnesses on his behalf present in Court. The witnesses for the prosecution were a Detective Inspector, two Detective Sergeants and a Detective Constable. In addition the Clerk of the Court, according to newspaper reports at the time, was very belligerent, hectoring John Anderson and contradicting him. Anderson pleaded not guilty, and was remanded to the Assizes.

CHAPTER FIVE
Derby Assizes

The next stage of the trials was at the Derby Assizes and took place on July 21st and July 22nd – sixty miles from the homes of the ramblers. This made it absolutely impossible for the Defence to muster any witnesses, as the cost would now be very much higher, and would also have to include possible overnight hotel expenses. On this occasion only Tony Gillet and John Anderson were legally represented, the remainder of the ramblers not being too happy at the manner in which legal representatives had acted in the Lower Courts.

It would appear, however, that even the K.Cs. were not sufficiently alert to challenge the make-up of the Grand Jury. The comments made by Ted Rivers who had researched the trial in the journal 'The Progressive Rambler' for April 1942 best sums up the matter. He wrote, 'The most remarkable feature of the trial was the composition of the Grand Jury (Grand is certainly the word). Here were six ramblers charged with offences connected with walking on a piece of land which in the past had been stolen from the people by grasping landowners. Of what did this Grand Jury – that central feature of British justice – consist? Local grocers and candlestick makers perhaps? Certainly not. These ramblers were tried before a Jury consisting of two brigadier generals, three colonels, two majors, three captains, two aldermen and eleven country gentlemen'.

We also found that the charges against us had been altered. Previously the main charge had been that of 'unlawful assembly'. We now found that the charge stated 'They riotously assembled together, and that they riotously assembled together and assaulted Edward Beever'. In addition I was charged with inciting various persons to riot and assault. John Anderson was additionally charged with occasioning actual bodily harm.

The whole apparatus of the state was now brought to bear to intimidate the ramblers, and through them, the rambling public.

The pomp and ceremony of the bewigged judges and barristers in their medieval robes, the atmosphere in court with police, ushers, and now with prison warders in attendance, all cast a threatening atmosphere over the proceedings.

Even before the hearing I had been receiving some private intimidation. In the week prior to the hearing my home had been visited by 'officials' who claimed that they were from Strangeways Prison. They wanted to know how often I went out during the week, who my companions were, and all about me. Unfortunately, I was not present when these alleged 'officials' arrived, or I should have tried to find out who they really were and the purpose of their enquiries. They didn't frighten me, but they certainly frightened my mother and sisters. Another little incident in the early part of the trial shows the malice of the Judge, Sir Edward Acton, and the cavalier manner in which he tried to squash and belittle us. Owing to the fact that we were strangers in Derby and had difficulty in finding a reasonable cafe near the Court for a drink and sandwich during the dinner interval, five of us were ten minutes late in arriving back. Justice Acton really went to town. He could not have been more vicious. He did not give us the opportunity to explain, or apologise. He put on an act of outraged indignation and stormed and raged about 'contempt of Court'. He told us that for this 'contempt' we would be kept in custody overnight, a further intimidation. It gave us a taste of things to come, a night in the cells at Leicester Jail with all the bombast and bullying of prison discipline with no opportunity for a discussion of the day's and next day's proceedings between the men on trial.

In my case I was not even allowed a light in my cell so that I could write up comments on the evidence which had been presented for my final defence submission. Still, it solved the problem for us of where to stay overnight without further expense.

The following day the prosecution team of police and keepers, well briefed and rehearsed, now word perfect from their previous court appearances, were called and made their statements.

Minor items of interest were squeezed out of the witnesses in the course of cross-examination. A Detective Inspector dealt with the events before the Trespass. His main purpose was to show the fear and apprehension in Hayfield caused by the proposed Trespass, in order to establish the element in the charge that alarm was actually caused by the Trespass. He stated that he had received complaints in writing about the proposed Trespass, but would not reveal who the people were who complained, then made a monumental blunder by stating they were mainly 'people who own the land'. That statement was the heart of the prosecution's case. It was the landowners who were afraid of the consequences of the Mass Trespass, and of the philosophy of mass action. Hence the trial. We had to be squashed, ramblers had to be taught a lesson, that behaviour of this kind would not be tolerated by the establishment.

Among other charges against me, was one of inciting various persons to riot and assault. This was a very serious matter. The main prosecution witness for this charge was a Detective Sergeant. He had been present at the meeting in the quarry and quoted in great detail statements which he alleged I had made, but he had written nothing down at the time, and was quoting from memory. Alas for him, he could not remember the words I actually used to 'incite the crowd to violence'. With more pressure from me he admitted that I had called for a disciplined, quiet and orderly demonstration, with no incitement to violence.

Justice Acton, true to tradition, did cause some merriment in Court and at the same time instil prejudice into the case. A 'damning' piece of evidence been presented. Tony Gillett was found to have in his possession, when arrested, a book by Lenin. To great laughter His Lordship asked, 'Isn't that the Russian gentleman?'.

Trespassers and keepers.

Then came my defence. I made a nine page statement giving the history of the struggle for access to mountains and the policy of the B.W.S.F. and finally dealt with the Trespass itself. On the battle with the keepers I commented that 'there is only evidence from one witness of a blow being struck, and that is from a keeper who alleges he was struck with a buckle of a belt'. I pointed to the contradictory evidence of all the witnesses to the scuffle where Beever sprained his ankle and received a stomach injury, with the number of ramblers ranging from a 'howling mob of 100 to 150' and to '12 to 20' and a statement concerning a 'general attack on Beever, dragging him downhill', with no witnesses actually having seen a single blow struck'.

I commented that it seemed obvious that Beever started a scuffle with one rambler and a crowd of ramblers gathered around watching. I pointed out that the ramblers had no hesitation in returning to Hayfield. I asked, 'would a gang of hooligans who had just indulged in a general riot, have returned to a small village which they knew was packed with police?' Dave Nussbaum, John

The injured keeper.

43

Whether the crowd were trespassing or not was immaterial, but it might be material that the crowd were told they were trespassing.

This was the remark made by Mr. Justice Acton at Derby Assizes to-day when the hearing was resumed of the case in which six Manchester youths are charged with riotous assembly and assault at Hayfield, in the Peak district.

Anderson, Tony Gillett, Jud Clyne and Harry Mendel, all pleaded not guilty to the charges.

The Judge took two hours in summing up, first of all directing that Harry Mendel should be discharged through lack of evidence. Justice Acton then said that no other country had such freedom of procession and demonstration as ours, and nobody would wish to see a curtailment of these rights, but the object of the prosecution was to prevent such things being done in a manner that amounted to a riot or unlawful assembly, and to strike terror in people's breasts.

The Jury was absent for three quarters of an hour to decide their verdict. John Anderson was found not guilty of causing grievous bodily harm but guilty of assaulting Beever. I was found guilty of riotous assembly together with the rest of the boys and guilty of incitement to riotous assembly, but I was found not guilty of incitement of various persons to riot and assault. The sentences ranged from six months for John Anderson, four months for me, two months each for Tony Gillett and Jud Clyne, three months for Dave Nussbaum – one month more than Tony Gillett because he was found guilty of the very serious crime of selling the Daily Worker! Harry Mendel was discharged.

Before passing sentence on Tony Gillett, Justice Acton, by obvious arrangement with the defence barrister, mildly reprimanded Tony for having become involved in 'such an unsavoury event'. Then came the moment of truth, the prepared question, 'aren't you ashamed of what you did?' he asked. It was obvious to me that Tony had merely to offer some form of apology, in order to receive a reprimand and to be dismissed with a warning about his future conduct. That was something Tony was not prepared to do. He drew himself up to his full height, and looked the Judge full in the face. 'No Sir, I would do it again' he answered. So the best laid plans of the defence counsel came to nothing. Tony Gillett was sentenced to two months like Jud Clyne.

We were now the property of the prison service, taken down to the cells of the Assize Courts, and later transported by Black Maria to Leicester Jail. That seemed to be the end of the Mass Trespass. Or was it?

CHAPTER SIX
Not in Vain

The immediate reaction from the rambling public, from lovers of
the open air, and from the public at large, was a greater awareness
of the injustice of the situation and the need for access to
mountains. Frank Turton, a prominent Sheffield figure in the
open air movement, stated 'thousands of ramblers went to view
the scene of the Mass Trespass. National interest was aroused as
never before.' The annual demonstration of ramblers at Winnats
Pass, Castleton, on June 26th 1932 (that was even before the Derby
Assizes were held, and the sentences passed) brought an
attendance of ten thousand ramblers – the biggest number in its
history. A further Mass Trespass was held in Derbyshire at Abbey
Brook in the Derwent Valley. Another, along Stanage Edge on
October 16th, was stopped by mounted police and foot patrols
with Alsatian dogs (unprecedented at the time). A protest rally
was held at Jacob's Ladder, at which Jud Clyne, among others,
spoke. In the South a thousand-strong demonstration in support
of access was held at Leith Hill, Surrey. Later, rallies for access
were held both in Scotland and Wales.

*Above & Below: The protest rally at Jacob's
Ladder August 1932.*

Dr. C. E. M. Joad addressing 10,000 ramblers.
at the Access to Mountains meeting in Winnats
Pass in June 1932.

Kinder Downfall

Edale Cross

In spite of their opposition to the Mass Trespass, the Manchester Ramblers' Federation officials, 'after careful consideration of all the circumstances' to use their own words, wrote to the Home Secretary appealing for the exercise of clemency 'not only as an act of grace, but on the grounds of public policy'. Many other Ramblers' Federations in the country followed the example of the Manchester Federation and protested. The Home Secretary answered that he could find no grounds for any remission of sentences. A flame had been lit and things could never be quite the same again. Time after time in negotiations with landowners they were reminded of the Mass Trespass when they were trying to kill negotiation by procrastination.

It is interesting to note that fifty-six percent of all moorland and mountains to which the public now have access under The National Parks and Access to the Countryside Act of 1949, is in the Peak District. The first and largest National Park in Britain was the Peak District National Park. This was no accident. The history of struggle for access, the years of battles with gamekeepers and landowners, culminating in the Mass Trespass onto Kinder and the ensuing trespasses in Derbyshire, left their mark on the landowners and legislators. It made the position of the ramblers' negotiators much stronger. The Mass Trespass was not in vain.

It is easy now, after fifty years, to look back and see the mistakes made by the Mass Trespass organisers. We should never have antagonised the leadership of the Ramblers' Federation and those rambling leaders who had worked hard over a long period of time. We should perhaps have used our youthful zeal and energy inside the rambling movement, but of course, the faults were not all on one side.

Even today there are those in the rambling movement who stubbornly can see nothing good in the struggles which took place, and who close their eyes and minds to the tremendous impetus given to the struggle for access to the mountains by the Mass Trespass. Access to mountains as envisaged by the pioneers has still not been achieved. The Access to the Countryside Act of 1949 goes some way towards it, but there are still vast tracts of mountain and moorland in Britain not covered by access agreements. New problems like the ploughing up of moorland, exploration for minerals, and proposed reopening of long disused mines in beauty spots and green belts arise from time to time. In Even today, after years of negotiation, plans for access can still be rejected. In this continuing effort to achieve unrestricted freedom to explore areas of outstanding natural beauty the lessons of the Mass Trespass over Kinder must never be forgotten.

Arthur Henderson MP speaking at the 1933 Winnats Pass Meeting. Bert Ward is on the extreme left of the photograph and Geoffrey Manders MP is in the middle with the walking stick.

Above: The Boxing Glove Stones, Kinder
Opposite: Kinder Reservoir
Overleaf: Grindsbrook

*The design of the Plaque by Peter Senior
unveiled April 1982 to commemorate the 50th
anniversary of the Kinder Trespass.*